Faster, Easie
THE WORLD
OF INVENTIONS

by ERIC OATMAN

Editorial Offices: Glenview, Illinois • Parsippany, New Jersey • New York, New York

Sales Offices: Needham, Massachusetts • Duluth, Georgia • Glenview, Illinois
Coppell, Texas • Sacramento, California • Mesa, Arizona

Changing the Way America Works

Until the early 1800s most families in the United States lived on farms and were self-sufficient. This means that they grew their own food, spun their own thread, and wove their own cloth. They bought only what they were unable to make—tools, shoes, and some furniture, for example. Blacksmiths, cabinetmakers, and other craftspeople manufactured special items such as these in small workshops.

Around 1820 factories began to appear in the northeastern states. New machines could turn out many products more quickly and more cheaply than people could make them at home. Over the next fifty years, setting up and running businesses and factories—a process called **industrialization**—changed the way Americans lived and worked.

Some of the earliest factories were cotton mills, where machines made thread and cloth. **Hydropower** made the machines run. Swift flowing rivers and streams turned water wheels, and hour after hour, the turning wheels kept the machines going.

The new factories were like magnets. By 1836 more than twelve thousand young women, raised on farms, had relocated to Lowell, Massachusetts. They moved there to work in the cotton mills. They lived in rented rooms and labored thirteen hours a day every day except Sunday. It was hard work, but many enjoyed the changes in their lives. They liked being away from home and earning more than two dollars a week— excellent pay in those days.

Teenagers and young women left their families' farms to work long hours in cotton mills.

Changes in Farming Methods

To grow one hundred bushels of wheat in 1830, a farmer with five acres of land had to work three hundred hours. In 1987 a farmer could raise one hundred bushels on three acres of land with only three hours of work.

What made this possible? Inventions did. An **invention** is a new machine or new way of doing something. Inventors built machines that helped farmers work faster and accomplish more. Four important examples of inventions that improved farming methods are shown in the time line.

Before 1920 at least one out of every two Americans worked on farms. Today only one in fifty Americans do. Yet, incredibly, America's farms are now producing more food than ever in history.

ractors help farmers pull
eavy equipment much more
asily than they ever could
y hand or with the help of
orses. They also help farmers
over a large field quickly.

arm Inventions 1780–1900

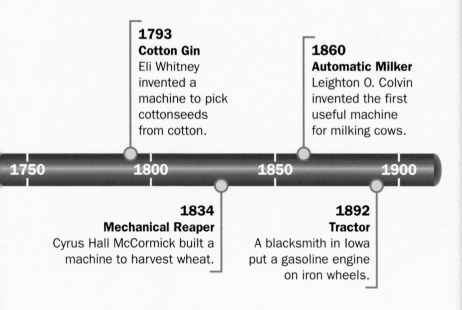

1793
Cotton Gin
Eli Whitney
invented a
machine to pick
cottonseeds
from cotton.

1860
Automatic Milker
Leighton O. Colvin
invented the first
useful machine
for milking cows.

1750   1800   1850   1900

1834
Mechanical Reaper
Cyrus Hall McCormick built a
machine to harvest wheat.

1892
Tractor
A blacksmith in Iowa
put a gasoline engine
on iron wheels.

The Age of Electricity

Thomas Edison was the first American to invent a light bulb that did not burn out quickly. In 1879 he held a New Year's Eve party to show off his invention. About three thousand people visited Edison's house and laboratory in Menlo Park, New Jersey. Electric lights glowed all around the property, and the visitors were amazed. Edison told them they would be able to discard their smelly kerosene lanterns and dangerous gas lamps in the years ahead.

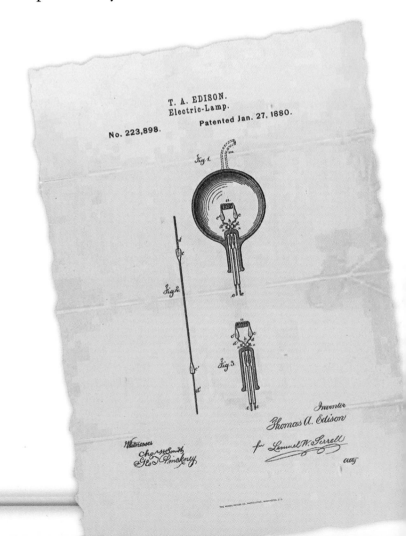

In the late 1800s Edison supervised the construction of a coal-fired electric power plant in New York City. Underground wires carried the electricity into homes and offices. Factories could now stay open all night.

Stringing wires long distances was expensive. As a result, homes in **urban** areas got electricity first. Many homes in **rural** areas, which were not as densely populated as cities, had no electricity until the 1940s.

Today it is hard to imagine life without electricity. What would we do without radios and motion pictures that were invented in the 1890s? What if our towns and cities had no traffic lights that were invented in 1914? Electricity is such an important part of modern life that electric companies have had to build power plants all across the nation.

Thomas Edison prepared this drawing for the United States Patent Office, which— even today—continues to give inventors the sole right to make and sell their inventions.

The Rise of Transportation

During the 1800s the need to get goods to market created a growing need for transportation. The **steamboat** and the canal boat helped move people and goods over water, and new roads helped link cities and towns over land.

In 1830 a New York inventor named Peter Cooper pieced together a steam locomotive called the *Tom Thumb*. It carried more than two dozen passengers at an average speed of ten miles an hour. By 1869 trains were crisscrossing the nation from New York to California.

New ideas about transportation came to light when automobiles appeared. The first cars ran on steam or electric batteries, and the first car owners tended to be wealthy. That changed in 1908, when Henry Ford built the Model T car. This new car was cheap, sturdy

nd easy to drive and repair. About fifteen million
people in the United States bought a Model T in the
nineteen years it was in production.

Airplanes transformed travel too. In 1903 the first
motor-powered plane took off from a sand dune in
Kitty Hawk, North Carolina. Its first flight lasted for
only twelve seconds. Today's jumbo jets can stay aloft
for fourteen hours without refueling.

The changes in transportation reinvented the
nation's economy. Farmers grew more, because trains
could haul their crops hundreds of miles to markets.
Roadside motels sprang up to accommodate travelers.
Increases in car ownership and roadways also led to
suburbs, shopping malls, and new businesses. The
businesses provided employment for pilots, mechanics,
truck drivers, road builders, and millions of others.

Automobile races, which started in the
United States in 1895, boosted people's
interest in owning cars—especially fast ones.

Faster Communication

From April 1860 to October 1861, young men on horseback carried mail back and forth between Missouri and California. Riding for the Pony Express paid well—one hundred dollars a month—but the job had no future. Once telegraph wires were strung from the East Coast to the West Coast, horses could not compete. Telegrams were expensive to send, but no horse traveled faster than the time it took a message to travel though the wires.

Trains were faster than horses, and telegrams were faster than trains. Inventions such as these made the world seem smaller.

Like other means of information exchange, or **communication**, the telegraph (invented in 1837) made the world seem smaller. It allowed people separated by thousands of miles to communicate more easily.

After Alexander Graham Bell invented the telephone in 1876, the world seemed to shrink even more. Wires connecting homes and offices allowed people to hold actual conversations over long distances.

Then in 1894 the Italian inventor Guglielmo Marconi transmitted Morse code signals over the air. His "wireless" later came to be called radio, and the world's first radio station–KDKA in Pittsburgh, Pennsylvania–gave the first voice broadcast in 1920.

The Internet Era

Tim Berners-Lee is one of the most significant inventors of the last hundred years. Over a two-year period, from 1989 to 1991, he invented the World Wide Web. The "Web" is a system that lets people share the information kept in computers.

The Web and the Internet are not the same thing. The Internet is a network of electronic "highways." The Web is like a chain of electronic trucks that carry words, sound, and pictures over that network.

The Internet was invented in 1969. Scientists used it to send e-mail to each other and to share collections of information called databases.

Berners-Lee opened up the Internet to millions of people. He did it by writing five kinds of **computer software**. One set of instructions made it possible to put Web sites on the Internet. Another gave these Web sites addresses, or URLs. Two others let people move documents between computers and browse, or surf, the Web.

Tim Berners-Lee invented the World Wide Web in the late 1980s. He and other software writers have been improving it ever since.

You can use the World Wide Web to find information about almost anything—from a recipe for gazpacho to the winners of the 1918 World Series.

The fifth program made servers work. Servers are computers that stay on all the time. They store databases and serve them to users who want to access the databases. Worldwide, there are millions of servers.

The Web caught on fast. Nearly one million people around the globe went online in 1991. At that time almost all of them used it for e-mail, for which the Web is not needed. In 2003 thanks to the Web, nearly six hundred million people had Internet access.

Surfing the Web can be entertaining. However, students who rely on it for help with research and homework are also aware of its value as an educational tool. The Web lets people tap into sources of information faster and more easily than ever before.

The Five Most Important Inventions in the United States

Inventions change lives. Nothing makes that clearer than a survey taken by researchers at the University of Florida in 1999. They asked Americans which inventions had the greatest impact on their lives. Here are the top five responses:

1. Computers

2. Television

3. Refrigerators

4. Medical Advances

5. The Internet

The invention of each of these items has a long history. The ancestry of computers stretches back to an Englishman named Charles Babbage (1791–1871). In 1833 he began to design an "analytical engine." His plan, which was never finished, was to build a machine to solve complicated math problems.

Twentieth-century inventors helped make food safer and more convenient to store and created new sources of entertainment and information.

Television had many parents, starting with the invention of the photoelectric cell in 1913 and the invention of both mechanical and electronic televisions in 1923.

The first refrigeration machine was invented in 1805, but home refrigerators did not begin entering American kitchens until 1916. In 1920 refrigerators were in about twenty thousand homes. By 1936 two million families in the United States owned one.

The average life expectancy of Americans born in 1900 was forty-nine years. Americans born in 2000 can expect to live an average of seventy-seven years. New medicines, devices like the MRI (magnetic resonance imaging), inventive surgical procedures, and other medical innovations are responsible for most of these gains.

Experts call the world we live in today "the information age." The Internet, the home of the World Wide Web, is one of the major reasons why.

Glossary

communication the way that people send and receive information

computer software programs that help computers perform certain functions

hydropower power produced by capturing the energy of flowing water

industrialization the creation of businesses and factories in a country or region

invention a new machine or new way of doing something

rural in small towns or farms

steamboat a boat powered by a steam engine

urban in the city